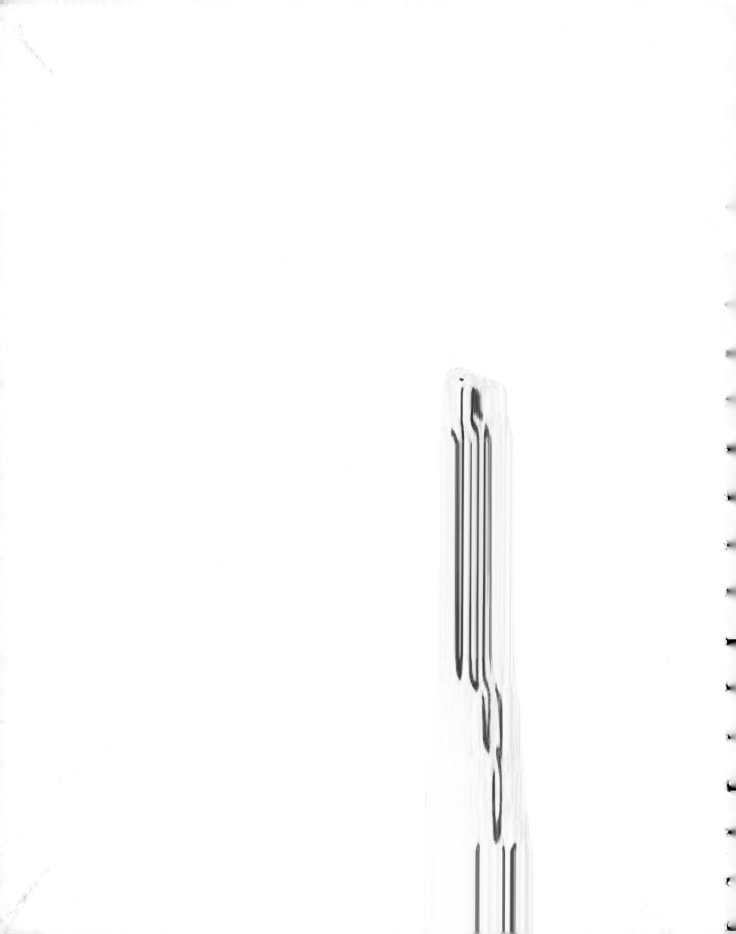

You Can't See a Dodo at the Zoo

WRITTEN BY
Fred Ehrlich

WITH PICTURES BY
Amanda Haley

BLUE APPLE BOOKS

To Marvin Krims, an endangered species,
but then so are we all.
—f.m.e.

Text copyright © 2005 by Fred M. Ehrlich
Illustrations copyright © 2005 by Amanda Haley
All rights reserved
CIP Data is available.
First published in the United States 2005 by
🍎 Blue Apple Books
515 Valley Street, Maplewood, N.J. 07040
www.blueapplebooks.com
First published in paperback by Blue Apple Books 2007
Distributed in the U.S. by Chronicle Books
First Paperback Edition
Printed in China

ISBN 13: 978-1-59354-624-3
ISBN 10: 1-59354-624-6

1 3 5 7 9 10 8 6 4 2

CONTENTS

INTRODUCTION

Once upon a time there were a lot of dodo birds. Now there are none. Dodos are extinct. Many other creatures are also extinct. Some died out many years ago. We know about them because we have found bones or fossils. Often we don't know what happened to these creatures; we don't know why they did not survive.

Other living things died out more recently. We know about them because people wrote descriptions or drew pictures of them. We even have photographs of some that died out after cameras were invented.

An animal is officially extinct when it has not been seen for fifty years. Every category of living thing has experienced extinction. Insects, birds, reptiles, mammals, amphibians, plants—there are many animals from each group that are no longer here on earth. Right now living things are dying out all the time.

Some animals are classified as "endangered." This means that few of them are still living and those that are alive are having trouble surviving. They may soon become extinct.

Oh, you can't see a dodo at the zoo.
You can look until your face is turning blue.
Even if it makes you mad,
Or very, very sad,
You still can't see a dodo at the zoo.

Oh, you can't see a woolly mammoth at the zoo.
It doesn't really matter what you do.
They lived in days of old
When it was very, very cold.
No, you can't see a woolly mammoth at the zoo.

Oh, you can't see a saber-toothed tiger at the zoo.
Because there aren't three, or even two.
In spite of scary teeth,
Every one has come to grief.
No, there is no saber-toothed tiger at the zoo.

Oh, you can't see
   a tyrannosaurus at the zoo.
Just as well because
   he would surely frighten you.
If he took one little bite,
You would disappear from sight.
No, there's **no tyrannosaurus**
   at the zoo!

CHAPTER ONE
dinosaurs

Dinosaurs lived so long ago that no person ever saw one. There are lots of pictures of dinosaurs. But these are just guesses made by artists and scientists. They may be good guesses, but they are guesses nonetheless.

All the information that scientists and artists have for their drawings comes from fossils. Fossils are the remains or impressions of plants and animals that have been preserved in the earth's crust. Scientists who study fossils are called paleontologists.

Paleontologists have found dinosaur bones, dinosaur eggs, dinosaur footprints, and dinosaur poop, which scientists call dung. The fossils came from dinosaurs that were covered by mud millions of years ago and little by little turned into stone.

Usually the soft parts, like skin, eyes, and insides, rotted away. Only the hard parts turned into fossils. It's not clear how dung could become fossilized since it was certainly soft.

Dino
Dung
8,000,000
BC

At one time there were many, many dinosaurs living all over the world. There were many different types: so far scientists have named around 860. They came in different sizes. Some were as small as chickens; others weighed many tons.

We know there must have been a lot of them, because we have found lots of fossils, and most dinosaurs did not turn into fossils when they died.

What happened to the dinosaurs? There are many theories. Here are just a few of them:

THE IMPACT THEORY
A giant meteorite hit the earth, raising so much dust that the sun could not heat the earth. Most living things froze or starved.

THE DISEASE THEORY
A germ infected the dinosaurs and killed them off.

THE SMALL ANIMAL THEORY
Small animals with sharp teeth ate the dinosaur eggs.

THE CLIMATE CHANGE THEORY
Over millions of years, the earth got colder. Since plants couldn't grow well, the dinosaurs didn't have enough to eat.

When there are so many different guesses, you can be certain that no one knows for sure what happened to the dinosaurs.

No one ever sawr a dino-sawr
Awr even what the dino-sawr sawr.
'Cause they aren't living anymawr.
They all died out so long befawr,
We don't know what the dino-sawr sawr.

No one ever heard a dino rawr,
Because there are none anymawr.
Were they mute? Did they snawr?
Did they dig up the forest flawr?
I'd like to hear a dino-sawr rawr!

TYRANNOSAURUS REX *a.k.a. Tyrant Lizard*

Tyrannosaurus Rex was the biggest flesh-eating animal that has ever existed. Tyrannosaurus weighed roughly five to seven tons.

**Old Tyrannosaurus
Won't ever sing for us**

BRACHIOSAURUS

This dinosaur ate only plants and was the largest land creature ever. The blue whale is larger, but it lives in the ocean.

**Brachiosaurus stamps its feet.
It wants a dozen trees to eat.**

SALTOPUS a.k.a. *Leaping Foot*

We usually think of dinosaurs as large, but this one was the size of a cat. Being small made it easier for saltopus to hide from bigger dinosaurs that wanted to eat it. Just as there are advantages to being the biggest, there are also advantages to being the smallest!

"Saltopus, saltopus, where have you been?"
"I have been hiding in order to win."

TRICERATOPS a.k.a. *Three-horn Face*

Triceratops may be the most famous dinosaur. It appears more often in dinosaur pictures than any other dinosaur. This may be because it looks so fierce.

Triceratops may be famous,
But it knows not what its name is!

DEINONYCHUS *a.k.a. Terrible Claw*

This dinosaur was about the size of a man. Its skeleton suggests it was a speedy runner. Its terrible claws probably made it a dangerous hunter.

Deinonychus
Doesn't look like-us.

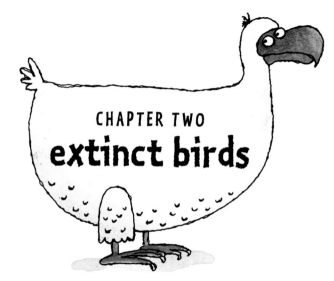

CHAPTER TWO
extinct birds

DODO

Dodos have been extinct for about three hundred years. They did not have the advantage that most birds have because they could not fly. They lived on the Mascarene Islands off the coast of Madagascar.

Early travelers hunted the dodos. They also brought pigs, cats, and rats to the islands. These animals ate the eggs and the young birds.

Dodos weighed up to 50 pounds and had beaks 9 inches long. None of us will ever see one.

**Dodos lived near Madagascar.
Your mom may not know where that is,
so you'd better not ask her!**

REUNION SOLITAIRE *a.k.a. White Dodo*

The white dodo lived on Reunion Island, next to where the dodo lived. When Bary de Saint Vincent visited the island in 1801, he was told that no white dodos had been seen for many years.

We know about this bird from a few paintings and written descriptions.

Pity the poor white dodo.
It posed for a painting,
but never a photo.

MOA

Moas, like dodos, were flightless birds. They lived in New Zealand millions of years ago in the Miocene or Pliocene eras.

Over time the climate of New Zealand became much wetter and the grasslands that the moas needed turned into forests.

Mama moas couldn't fly.
Baby moas wondered why.

LAYSON HONEYEATER *a.k.a. Redbird*

In 1923 the Tanoger Expedition of the U.S. Biological Society went to the Layson Island. They saw three of these birds. Since then, none have been seen.

It is thought that rabbits, introduced to Layson Island in 1903, ate the plants that these birds needed to survive.

Honeyeaters needed
flowers with honeys.
But the flowers were eaten
by families of bunnies.

19

Mommy, Mommy, I just heard
The singing of a dodo bird.

Johnny, Johnny, that's absurd!
You cannot hear an extinct bird.

I heard it, Mommy, in a dream.
It sounded something like a scream.

What good luck, Johnny, to have heard
The calling of an extinct bird.

CHAPTER THREE
extinct mammals

After the extinction of the dinosaurs, mammals evolved as the dominant large animals on the earth. Many of them looked a lot like the animals we know today.

A mammal is an animal with fur or hair that gives birth to live young, then nurses them.

As with other animals, mammals that became extinct could not find enough food or water, or the climate changed, or they could not protect themselves from enemies. And so their numbers diminished until eventually there were no more of them.

Saber-toothed tigers, woolly mammoths, some types of bandicoots, and potoroos - all are extinct. None roam the earth anymore.

SABER-TOOTHED TIGER

These large cats are not closely related to today's tigers. Scientists who have studied them have interesting theories about how they lived.

Some think that they waited in hiding, leaped out at their prey, and used their teeth to make slashing wounds in the soft bellies of the animals they jumped on.

Saber-toothed tigers became extinct 11,000 years ago. They probably perished because of climate changes. Some of them died in tar pits. In 1913 paleontologists found the bones of 2,000 saber-tooths in a pit near Los Angeles, California. The tigers became stuck in the gooey tar and could not free themselves.

Saber-tooths hunted
Near and far,
But didn't have the sense
To stay out of the tar!

WOOLLY MAMMOTH

We know a lot about woolly mammoths, because these now-extinct animals were still around when humans arrived on the scene. This was long before people learned how to write, but not before they could draw.

There are cave paintings of woolly mammoths in France that almost certainly show that men hunted them. Also, since they lived in the Ice Age, some of them were frozen under the snow and have since been dug up. So we know what they really looked like. We don't have to guess as we do with the dinosaurs.

Mammoths that lived in days of old
Looked like elephants dressed for the cold.

BANDICOOT

The barred bandicoot still lives on the island of Tasmania. Many other kinds of bandicoots are extinct. They were killed by foxes, cats, and dogs. Others were killed by toxoplasmosis, a disease carried by cats. Many greater rabbit bandicoots were caught in traps that had been set for rabbits.

The barred bandicoot is terribly cute,
At night it likes to play.
It used to have dozens of small, furry cousins,
But now they are all gone away!

GILBERT'S POTOROO   a.k.a. Rat Kangaroo

John Gilbert, a naturalist, explored Australia. In 1840 he described a species of potoroo with a black tail and a black stripe running down its face. It became extinct in 1900. Scientists named this species for John Gilbert.

In Kalamazoo or Timbuktu,
You'll never see Gilbert, or his striped potoroo.

QUAGGA

The quagga is sometimes mistaken for a zebra because
it has stripes. But a quagga's stripes run only a little of
the way down its back, then fade out.

The quagga was named for the noise it made. Unfortunately,
it became extinct before we had recording machines,
so we can't really know what it sounded like.

> Eeney, meeney, miney, mo,
> Catch a quagga by the toe.
> If he hollers let him go,
> Eeney, meeney, miney, mo!

Hey! Wait a minute!
He can't holler...
he's dead as a dodo!

One night I thinked
Everything was extinct!
No dogs, no cats,
No rats, no bats.
The last animal's drink
had been drinked!

CHAPTER FOUR
endangered animals

Just because we say an animal is extinct doesn't always mean it is. It is very unlikely that there are dinosaurs alive anywhere, but when dinosaur fossils were first found, explorers went around the world looking for live ones.

In 1939 Marjorie Courtney-Latimer, a young curator at a museum in South Africa, was watching fishermen unload their catch. She spotted a five-foot-long, pale blue fish. She said, "This one definitely goes to the museum."

She drew a quick sketch and sent it off to South Africa's leading fish expert. He recognized it as a coelacanth—an animal thought to have been extinct for seventy million years!

Once we thought old coela was dead.
Now get that notion out of your head!

Endangered species are particularly interesting because we can actually see them. Even more important, sometimes we can figure out what is endangering them and try to do something about it.

There are endangered species in all categories of living things: plants, fish, mammals, insects, and birds. Many endangered creatures are familiar to most of us; even more are known to scientists. Every day they add new animals to the "endangered species" list.

MANATEE

The manatee is thirteen feet long and weighs two thousand pounds. It's a gray, slow-moving mammal that lives in the water. The main danger to the survival of the manatees is boats, which strike them in shallow waters and cut them with their propellers.

The manatee has a squishy snout
And big, fat flippers to paddle about.
Though it isn't pretty to you or me,
It is to another manatee.

WHOOPING CRANE

A beautiful, graceful, migrating bird, whooping cranes were never known to be plentiful. They are 52 inches tall, the tallest American bird. The whooping crane's loud call has been compared to a trumpet or a bugle.

When whooping cranes migrate from their nesting grounds in Canada to their winter quarters in Texas, they are in danger from coyotes and wolves, hunters, power lines, and storms.

They were nearly extinct in 1941 when only 21 of these birds could be found. Since 1958 there have been tremendous conservation efforts to save whooping cranes. Shooting them was made illegal, and their nesting grounds were protected. By 1990, 270 whooping cranes were counted.

Oh, a marvelous bird
Is the whooping crane.
It flies to Texas
And back again!

TASMANIAN DEVIL

A Tasmanian devil is a three-foot-long marsupial. It is short and stocky with a large, bear-like face. It has a pouch like a kangaroo, but the pouch opens from the bottom instead of from the top so that dirt doesn't get into the pouch when the devil crawls. You may wonder how the babies don't fall out. They just don't!

Tasmanian devils have powerful jaws, short strong limbs, and strong claws. By reputation they are extremely fierce and often kill sheep and other animals. One was said to have killed fifty-four chickens, six geese, an albatross, and a cat in two nights!

Because of their attacks on farm animals, Tasmanian devils were hunted to the point of extinction. However, when raised by humans, they can make good pets.

BLUE WHALE

The blue whale is the largest living creature on earth.
One whale can weigh more than thirty elephants.
A newborn whale calf weighs 2,000 pounds.

The whales are endangered because they are hunted for meat. In the past, they were hunted for their blubber, which was used to make oil for lamps.

Blue whale, blue whale,
How was it done?
You gave birth to a baby
Weighing close to a ton!

PIPING PLOVER

The piping plover is a shore bird that is in danger of becoming extinct. Its enemies are crows, gulls, and other large birds that eat plover eggs and baby plovers.

A park ranger at the Cape Cod National Seashore has the job of protecting piping plover nesting grounds on the beach. When she finds a nest, she puts a wire "house" over it. The house has an opening big enough to let the plovers come and go, but too small for the crows to get in and steal the eggs.

Park rangers and many others are fighting to protect endangered animals, but it's a complicated situation. On Cape Cod, crows are native birds, and so are plovers. They have shared the same area for thousands of years. So why is there trouble now?

Crows are very good at sharing their territory with humans. Plovers are not. When people walk on the beaches where plovers nest, they scare the adult birds away and the babies may die. So there are fewer plovers the next year.

If they don't find plover eggs to eat, crows will eat food left by people. And so there are more crows every year. More crows eat more plover eggs. So, despite help from rangers, there are fewer and fewer plovers.

Hunting plover eggs,
Ms. Crow is an explorer.
But the wily park ranger
Got to the nest before her!

THYLACINE *a.k.a. Tasmanian Tiger*

In Australia there is a National Thylacine Day. The thylacine (Tasmanian Tiger) was a large, dog-like, meat-eating marsupial. The last one sighted for certain was in 1936. That is more than fifty years ago, and as you know, when an animal hasn't been seen for fifty years, it is officially extinct.

So why are we calling this animal endangered? Officially it is gone, but several people have reported seeing one. Now there is a hunt on to find thylacines and to move this animal from "extinct" to "endangered," just like the coelacanth.

Some people say they saw one;
Other people doubt it.
Some scream, "They're not extinct!"
"Well, you needn't shout about it!"

CONCLUSION

I once saw two coyotes walking down a road on Cape Cod in Massachusetts. I asked a park ranger what the coyotes were doing on the road.

"They're doing the same thing you are," he said. "It's easier for them to walk on the road than to struggle with the cat briars in the woods."

It is hard for us to see the world from the point of view of all the other creatures on earth. We drive along and wonder at the dead raccoons, squirrels, and deer. What were they doing on the highways?

But the woods and meadows and their inhabitants were there before the highways. The animals used all the paths and spaces. They did not learn to stay out of the way of cars as they went about their business.

We need roads, and towns, and farms, and factories. But most creatures cannot live where we do. What we can do, however, is be aware that every change we make affects other living creatures. Then we can make responsible decisions about how we can take care of ourselves while doing the least harm to other living things.

GLOSSARY

amphibian: cold-blooded vertebrate that lives on land but breeds in water; babies can live in water, then grow to live on land

bird: warm-blooded, egg-laying vertebrate characterized by feathers and wings

conservation: the protection and preservation of wildlife

curator: a person who works at an art or natural history museum

dung: animal poop

endangered: an animal that is in close danger of extinction

expedition: a group of people going on a journey for a particular purpose

extinct: no longer existing or living

fossil: an impression of a plant or animal that existed in a past geological age

Ice Age: any period of time during which glaciers covered a large part of the earth's surface

mammal: any warm-blooded vertebrate having the skin more or less covered with hair; young are born alive and nourished with milk

marsupial: mammals of which the females have a pouch containing the teats where the young are fed and carried

meteorite: a stony or metallic mass of matter that has fallen to the earth's surface from outer space

Miocene Era: the time period 13 to 25 million years ago during which grazing mammals first appeared on earth

native: an animal or plant that originated in a particular place or region

paleontologist: a person who specializes in the study of the forms of life existing in prehistoric or geologic times

Pliocene Era: the time period 2 to 13 million years ago during which mountains developed, the climate cooled, and more and larger mammals appeared

reptile: a cold-blooded animal that crawls or moves on its belly or by means of small, short legs

species: a class of animals whose members can have babies together

theory: a set of statements or principles offered to explain natural phenomena